If the Souls Could Speak

By Michael J. Maxson

365 Souls Have Come Calling

You can read this book in just a day,
but it will be with you for a lifetime.

PRESS

If the Souls Could Speak
365 Souls Have Come Calling
by Michael J. Maxson

Printed in the United States of America

ISBN 9781609578626

Unless otherwise indicated, Bible quotations are taken from The New International Version of the Holy Bible. Copyright © 1986 by Holman Bible Publishers.

All quotes and pictures that are not duly noted are from the author.

Photo editing provided by Hannah Julianne Photography.

Front Cover: Bennett Cemetery established in 1700's, located in Wadesboro, NC.

Back Cover: Quaker Burying Ground, established 1759, located in Camden, SC.

www.xulonpress.com

With all the differences of opinion in the world; from politics,
to religion, to race relations, there is one thing we all have
in common: we are all going to die–at least physically.
This book is a means to prepare us for that inevitable
outcome. In understanding this reality, it is my hope
that the words contained herein will bring the
world a bit closer to embracing the
ultimate power of love.

The one thing I have come to know and be accountable to is
the full understanding of the reality of the invisible,
eternal, spiritual world of goodness and evil.
It is our choice to which we connect.

I don't know how much time I have, and with that consciousness,
I give you my very best.

Michael J. Maxson

CONTENTS

Endorsements

If the Souls Could Speak prepares readers for the reality of death and facing the loss of loved ones, told through the first-person account of someone who's been there. It encourages readers to appreciate every moment of life and make the most of the time allotted to them. Most of all, it does what the title suggests: allows the voices of *"those gone by"* to speak through the inspiring words of their epitaphs.

—A.J. Kiesling, author of *Skizzer.*

For one who has greatly suffered the loss of loved ones, Mike Maxson has connected with his grief and met the challenge. *If the Souls Could Speak* is truly inspiring and provides you the tools to find peace, passion and renewed purpose in your own life.

—Ann Noonan: MS, Med., LPC, NCC; founder, therapist and Clinical Director - Agape' Christian Counseling.

What a tribute to life and our need to know our Savior. Great Job! A+!

—Harold Brubaker: Business Owner, North Carolina State Representative.

ACKNOWLEDGEMENTS

To my three children, Lindsay, Andy, and Hannah:

A blessed man am I that you are my three children. You're each different, yet perfect in your own way and carry within your hearts the love of Jesus Christ. There is no greater tribute for a parent than to say that about their kids. Your mother is proud of you and loves you, and so do I.

To Mary Ann:

Your loving and unshakeable faith provided me the inspiration and confidence to persist. When my faith was overshadowed by doubt, you continued to believe and made me feel worthy of God's love. I thank you for your devotion, your love, and most of all for who you are – a captivating spirit of God's loving kindness.

DEDICATION

This book is dedicated to Linda Julianne Maxson, a loving wife, mother, and friend, who met with an untimely death due to a condition called Deep Vein Thrombosis (DVT). DVT is a blood clot that forms in a deep vein and can be fatal if not treated. DVT is responsible for more deaths in the United States than breast cancer, AIDS, and traffic fatalities combined! (The Charlotte Observer, October 30, 2007)

In Linda's case, she had outpatient foot surgery and just a few days later experienced the textbook signs of a DVT, including severe calf pain. On several occasions she reported her condition to her surgeon, but the concerns were ignored. Nineteen days after sharing her symptoms, Linda died from a massive pulmonary embolism that began as a DVT.

It is my hope for this book to bring awareness to this condition. Two websites you can access to gain more knowledge are www.preventdvt.org and www.factorvleiden.org. I pray you take the time to review this information and become more prepared and empowered to help yourself and others.

If Linda's soul could speak today, she would encourage us to be more knowledgeable of the medical decisions surrounding our lives and not take for granted that the medical community has our best interest in mind.

Additionally, she would ask for us to be more loving, kind, and considerate, to say "please" and "thank you" more often, and to listen twice as much as we talk. She would want us to live one day at a time and to know that no one is guaranteed tomorrow. She would ask, "If today were your final day on earth, how would you be remembered?"

Thank you, Linda, for the love, kindness and joy you shared on a daily basis. To know you was a blessing and it was an honor to have been your husband. You were truly a gift from God and one who will always be remembered.

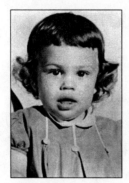

Kimberly Ann

Robert Charles (Shorty)

Harold James (Jim/Mac)

Gwendolyn (Gwen)

Linda Julianne

TRIBUTE

I would like to give tribute to the lives that provided the inspiration
for this writing. It was from their deaths that the clay was molded.

Kimberly Ann Maxson
11/27/57 – 3/22/61

Robert Charles Maxson
10/7/63 – 12/13/65

Harold James Maxson
4/8/27 – 5/10/97

Gwendolyn Maxson
7/17/31 – 2/13/03

Linda Julianne Maxson
2/7/52 – 3/2/05

As we write our own life story, may the spirits of those who
have briefly gone before us reach out and embrace our existence.
May their stories be remembered and touch our souls.
In doing so, our loved ones will live through us
and their story will be our story.

INTRODUCTION

Three Things We All Have

We all have three things in common: our birth, our life, and our death. Births are celebrated, life is taken for granted, and death is ignored—until it happens to us. One of the greatest issues of the world today is that people live in bodies that are going to die, but act as if they're not. From the time we are born, we are on a journey to our final frontier: physical death.

If the Souls Could Speak was written to give you a promise of hope. We all are going to die physically someday, and it is my intention to bring you to that understanding. This book is not for everyone, because many choose to ignore death.

For some, it is a very uncomfortable subject to think about, much less study. For others, they may read about someone in the local paper, or hear about an elderly relative passing, but it did not hit close to home and therefore had little impact. Death is something that will happen far in the future or to someone else, but not to "me."

The reality of life is that *you will* die one day, and if it is tomorrow, are you prepared today? This is a question that must be addressed. You can't do much about your birth, but you can certainly design a plan for your final day.

Death can come in different ways, from an extended illness to a sudden and unexpected episode. You could die in an accident, contract a disease, be killed while serving others, murdered by a criminal, commit suicide, die from old age, or be executed for a crime. You could experience the death of someone you love; such as a parent, sibling, spouse, child, relative, or friend – it could be anyone at any time. If we live for many years, we all will face the challenge of dealing with death's despair and sorrow at some point in your life.

If the Souls Could Speak prepares you for that ultimate reality. It is also a work of poetry, and once read, your life will never be the same. The writings found in the following pages represent some of the most powerful words you could ever read. They are words from families like yours who encountered the storm of death and, in their way, embraced eternity.

The unaltered words, chiseled in stone, were authored at a time of great emotion. Their statements of life and death are to be honored, understood, and embraced. Every syllable carries with it the music of God's eternal love, for it was God who gave us the words.

"When you were born, you cried and the world rejoiced.
When you die, the world will cry and you will rejoice."

Old Indian Saying

Chapter 1

A Little of My Story

The process of losing loved ones comes to us all sooner or later. As for me, I lost a sister when I was five, a brother when I was ten, a father when I was forty-two, a mother when I was forty-seven, and a wife when I was forty-nine. In my first fifty years of life God taught me five great lessons. I pray my next fifty will be filled with sharing what I have learned and paying forward God's love to others.

It is from their deaths that my soul has been united with God. Death is a vehicle by which lifeless souls can be reborn, and with it a fresh and inspired outlook on life can be realized. Very simply, when we lose a loved one our passion for life can deepen and a greater appreciation for the fact that we are still alive will surface.

At first it's very difficult to see the blessing in the death of someone you love deeply. The pain and sense of loss are overwhelming and you experience the rollercoaster of emotions such as grief, guilt, anger, loneliness, remorse, emptiness, sadness, and despair. These emotions can consume your soul, and you may demand an answer from God as to "why".

Why did my parents have to go through the terrible loss of not just one child, but two? Why did my wife's doctor completely ignore her obvious signs of a DVT and send her to an early grave? Why, why, why? We can cry this one-word prayer over and over again, searching for answers that may never come. Many of you reading this now are asking the same question about your loved one, and I understand; it is completely natural to do so, at least for a while.

You must, however, eventually come to understand that no matter how much you mourn and cry out for change, your loved one is not coming back (at least physically). Reaching this point of acceptance will allow you to move on to the next chapter in your life, and this certainly is what your loved one would want you to do.

If you could have one last conversation with your loved one, what would they say? What would they want you to hear? How would they want you to feel? "If the Souls Could Speak," What would they want you to know?

I promise, they would not want you to find comfort in your pain, nor continually beat yourself up because they are gone. They would not want you to idolize their life and thereby maintain that empty hole in your heart. They would not want you to use your sorrow as a way of remembrance and thus stifle the goodness of who they were.

They would not want you to continually say "if only" and "should have." These feelings of remorse, guilt, and regret are natural but very destructive. From a Christian perspective, they are tools of the evil one (a.k.a. the Adversary, Satan, Lucifer, or the Devil). Whatever you want to call it, this invisible, spiritual force is relentless and will do all it can to make you feel unworthy of any love, peace, or joy that may enter your life. I have had to battle these feelings of unworthiness, and so must you.

"God is great, you are good, and Satan can go to Hell! Amen."

Instead, your loved ones would want you to know they are at peace and happy with their new home in Heaven, and would want the same for you. They would want you to know:

"The depth of your pain has now expanded your ability to love and serve others."

They would want you to know the good memory of who they were is now your vehicle to make yourself better and thus make the world better. They would want you to embrace the understanding that the human race has a **100 percent mortality rate** and that their death simply occurred a little sooner than yours. They would want you to realize that your physical body is just a temporary earth suit that clothes your eternal spirit.

When you die physically, you are actually being transformed into an invisible, infinite, spiritual world of unlimited possibilities. We of the Christian faith call this place Heaven, and your loved one would want you to know that the first words you will say when you get there are, "Oh, now I understand!" It is then that your painful cries of *"why"* will be answered.

So until your time comes, just know there is a reason for why things happen, but it is not our place to get it all figured out. It is our place however, to embrace this wonderful thing we call life, seize its' opportunities to love and serve others, and make our loved one proud of the life we are now living.

Please look around, for you can always find someone who is being challenged with a difficult situation, perhaps one worse than yours. And when you do, simply hold their hand, listen to their pain and just let them know; *"Everything will be okay. I promise."*

"From the time we are born, till we are riding in a hearse;
nothing could be so bad, that it couldn't be worse."

Col. Glenn Coffey

Chapter 2

The Challenge

We last spoke around 2:45 p.m. on March 2, 2005, when I was traveling from Orangeburg, South Carolina, to Fayetteville, North Carolina. Linda had foot surgery a month earlier and I was staying in touch regularly to make sure she was doing okay. We had a good chat and discussed the following quote: *"Who we are is 99 percent invisible."* Fortunately, we had a good understanding that we are spiritual beings first and physical bodies second. Who would have ever known that would be our final conversation?

I arrived at my company's branch around 5 p.m. and made a quick call home again to check on her, only to have my neighbor answer the phone. Linda had suffered a fainting spell and was short of breath; an ambulance was on the way. I immediately began the three-hour drive home. During this time, I battled negative thoughts and finally came to the conclusion that she would be just fine.

I arrived at the hospital at the same time as my daughter Hannah and for over twenty minutes could not get any news on Linda's condition. Finally, we were escorted to a private room where the doctor informed us that Linda was in a "grave" condition. When a blood clot breaks loose, as in Linda's case, it then forms a Pulmonary Embolus (PE), and death can occur as a result of suffocation.

The doctor then led us to the emergency room where we found Linda motionless. Her eyes were already dilated and she was barely breathing. The doctor suggested trying to shock her heart for a third

24

time. With this offer of hope, we encouraged her: *"Come on, Linda, you can do it." "Please, Mommy, you can make it!"*

After a few seconds, we could see it didn't help and her life was fading. Our words then became, *"I love you, Linda." "I love you, Mommy."* With no other medical option available, I gave the doctor permission to end life support, and at 8:53 p.m. Linda Maxson's life came to an end. I can still hear Hannah's hysterical words as she ran out of the emergency room: *"My Mommy's dead! My Mommy's dead!"* The waiting room packed with friends erupted in shock and disbelief.

My body began shaking uncontrollably as the storm of death charged in like a tornado and I was thrown into the depths of despair and sorrow. A sense of loss, loneliness, and confusion consumed my soul, for my best friend and wonderful mother to my children was gone. My friends cried hysterically as we embraced and tried to connect with this reality. I'll never forget my buddy Johnny wrapping his strong arms around me and crying, *"This can't be happening!"*

Our lives were forever changed and I now had to make the painful calls to my oldest daughter and son. Lindsay was away at college in Wilmington, North Carolina, and Andy was completing his Air Force Reserves training in Texas. Their cries of horror on the phone are a nightmare I care not to revisit.

So please, allow Linda's tragic death to be a reminder for us all that **no one**, and I mean **no one**, is guaranteed tomorrow.

Chapter 3

After Passing

After Linda's passing, I visited her gravesite regularly searching for answers. My cries of *why* were painful and deep, for I had lost my best friend and partner of twenty-four years. I would spend quiet time cleaning her marker and asking God for help and direction. I soon found myself cleaning my neighbors' markers as well. This became a community project, for God revealed to me that we are all connected and a part of His spiritual community.

On one visit, I approached a family who was across the street visiting a fresh grave. It was the father, mother, and sister of a young man of twenty-six years who died suddenly. As we shared our stories, the father told me, *"My son was full of the Holy Spirit, but I did not know it…till now."* It was the loss of his son that brought the father to a deeper understanding of God's presence. It is from these challenging storms that our lives can be strengthened and a firm purpose discovered.

On another visit I met a gentleman whose gravesite was right beside mine. His wife had passed away a few days earlier, and he was hurting deeply. We talked a few minutes and exchanged stories. He then reached out his hand, introduced himself, and said, *"Well, I guess we need to get to know each other; after all, we will be neighbors one day."* Yes, we are all neighbors, and one day we will have a family reunion in heaven.

Today I don't visit Linda's grave as often, for my understanding of life has gained purpose. This process did not happen overnight, but was a day-by-day journey of digging deep within my soul for self-discovery, and after three years I am pleased to report to you that:

"My pain has been replaced with peace, my emptiness has been replaced with passion, and my confusion has been replaced with purpose."

I pray my words will bring you comfort and direction and take root in your heart. They are words from someone who has *"been there and done that."* I have lost almost everyone a person could humanly love, and the depths of my soul cry out for you to embrace my story.

Through the trials I have faced, my pain has been substituted for a relationship, and my effort to develop this connection has been my saving grace. And I pray the same for you. No matter your challenge—emotional, physical, or financial; whether it is drugs, alcohol, pornography, food, money, abuse, divorce, or yes, even the death of someone you love deeply—the storm that is rocking your boat can be calmed.

Just know that our true reward comes through a faith in Jesus Christ, who taught us the greatest lesson of all: eternal, spiritual life. Placing this first in your daily thoughts will take command of all your worries and life will be good. If I were to check out tomorrow, this is what I would want you to know today.

And when I say *"I am a Christian"*, that means I have studied and become a believer in the life, story, and teachings of the person we call Jesus Christ. As firmly documented in recorded history, He was a carpenter by trade, at age thirty began sharing His ministry on a full-time basis, and three years later, at age thirty-three, was executed for His teachings.

So profound was His life that the timeline which defines human existence as we know it today is based on His birth. Just this fact alone should warrant our most sincere consideration and study.

"There is no greater feeling on earth than having a personal connection with the love of Jesus Christ. He has been my saving grace."

Chapter 4

The Spark

Mary Ann and Mike at the gravesite in Easley, SC.
This is the marker that started it all - "The Spark."

On March 10, 2007, I was traveling on business and stayed overnight in Easley, South Carolina. After checking into my hotel, I had some daylight remaining and decided to go for a run. This is my time to relieve stress, think, and maintain some form of good physical condition. After all, I am alive and it is my responsibility to be as healthy as my self-discipline will allow. I was also still struggling with Linda's passing, and spending time with God at sundown is healing for me.

I left the hotel and found a route in a residential area. While on this course I passed a well-manicured cemetery tucked away in a field surrounded by houses on three sides. I circled the cemetery several times and on my last lap elected to enter the grounds. I had been in cemeteries before, but this visit changed my life. It wasn't long before I found the following words inscribed on one of the gravestones:

> *"Remember friends as you pass by,*
> *As you are now so once was I.*
> *As I am now, you soon will be.*
> *Prepare for death and follow me."*

After reading this, my life was introduced to a higher purpose. This quote ignited a passion to serve God as I have never experienced and ultimately led to the writing of this book. The key words referenced in the above quote are *"you soon will be."* We do not know when, where, or how, but what we do know is "soon" it will be. It could be tonight, tomorrow, next week, or next year. We all have that appointment with destiny and Linda is a vivid example of this reality. She was here one day and gone the next.

The second phrase to consider is *"prepare for death."* You *will* die someday, and when you do, will you be *"prepared"*? Most of us are not. Through my story and the epitaphs in this book, perhaps you too will embrace the reality of physical death and spiritual birth.

Your final day should be a day of celebration, and each day lived in preparation will empower your loved ones to carry on and live life greater than before. Your family and friends are your greatest legacy; so please prepare, for the future depends so much on what you leave behind.

> *"If you are prepared, you won't be scared."*

Allow me to share another situation that occurred on the day of Linda's passing. When I returned from the hospital around 11:30 p.m., my home was full of friends expressing their support. I could not find Hannah or Lindsay. Finally, I found them sitting on the floor in my bedroom closet, looking at pictures of their mom and crying their hearts out.

Let this be a lesson to us all. It is not the cars, the house, or the cash that will be meaningful on your final day; but rather the pictures you take, the letters you write, and the memories you make that will bring comfort to your loved ones.

Chapter 5

Who Will Write Your Epitaph?

Your epitaph, the permanent message you leave behind as a reminder to others, will be the landmark of your existence. It is your final "statement of life," which will be engraved in stone for all eternity to read. A select few will have the insight to prepare a message, while most of humanity will be blindsided by death and leave this task to family and friends.

As I have found, most of the modern graves (since the 1950s) have only the person's name and dates of birth and death inscribed. There are few poetic words to be found that give tribute to the life that was once vibrant and alive. It would be safe to say that since the invention of "human" electric power, our lives have been short-circuited from our connection with the "supreme" power. Television, the Internet, and a self-consumed lifestyle have allowed our society to become numb to our "spiritual" connection.

However, in the 1800s and early 1900s, families did not have these distractions and dealt directly with the extended illness or sudden death. Most did not live to ripe old ages, and many parents had to bury their children. There were very few hospitals to visit, florist shops to send flowers, or drugstores to buy a sympathy card, and it was common to die at home.

Life was simple then, but challenging, and families passed the test time and time again. This personal experience with death forced families to dig deep within their souls for answers. What they found was a loving God and a Savior named Jesus Christ, and it is often revealed on their headstones.

As in Linda's case, she did not choose the words for her epitaph, my kids did. She passed away suddenly on a Wednesday, and by Friday my kids and I were in a funeral home picking out a casket, gravesite, and headstone. To say we were not prepared for this is an understatement. We were still in shock and basically at the mercy and direction of the funeral director and his staff. Please let this be an example; get prepared ahead of time for you *do not* want to make these kinds of decisions under that level of emotional stress.

The process went as well as could be expected, and I know God had His hand in the decisions made. The funeral was on Sunday at Siler Presbyterian Church, and the family life center was at full capacity with over seven hundred in attendance. The outpouring of love and support was tremendous. My family was receiving back what Linda had been giving away for fifty-three years. Linda lived by the "Golden Rule," and the celebration of her life that day was a tribute to this principle.

We then traveled a few miles to Forest Lawn Cemetery; a beautiful location that Linda had indicated she would like to be buried one day, but had no idea it would become a reality so soon. The burial site had divine intervention, for Linda was laid to rest directly between Mandy Sage and Hope Stout.

Mandy was my daughter Lindsay's best friend, who died at age seventeen from an auto accident the day after senior prom. Hope Stout was a brave little girl of our community who died from cancer at age twelve and who had a tremendous impact on the Make-A-Wish Foundation. Linda loved children, and God symbolically placed her between two wonderful children and provided us with a permanent remembrance of her passionate calling of being a mom.

Though not prepared, my kids composed a message to their mom and for the world to read which simply stated, *"Love you mommy!"* Please hear me, moms and dads: *"Do you want to write your epitaph, or will you leave that job for your children?"*

"It's choice – not chance – that determines your destiny."

Jean Nidetch

Chapter 6

The Journey

Since that day in Easley, I now view cemeteries in a much different light. The opportunity to gather words of wisdom from these eternal resting places created in me a godly passion to serve. For two years I seized every opportunity to walk the grounds, gather the words, and share them.

With my occupation as a territory sales representative, I have had the privilege to travel the back roads of North and South Carolina, and from these travels I discovered many interesting and beautiful graveyards, especially the older ones. As mentioned earlier, it is in the older cemeteries that you will find the deeper wisdom and insight.

Unfortunately, many of the words inscribed on the older headstones are starting to fade. The winds of time are slowly erasing these profound words, and in a few more years they will be gone. It is so frustrating when I find a marker that I cannot read; yet at one time the inscription was sharp and the message clear.

It has been a distinct blessing that God gave me the vision to capture these words before they're gone. I have traveled thousands of miles, visited more than seventy towns, and walked for hours through graveyards searching for these powerful words. God only knows how many markers I studied. Some cemeteries had no words to offer, while others brought me to my knees.

This book contains 365 epitaphs, one for each day of the year. There were about 185 that I did not use, for a total of 550 quotes scribbled down on pocket pads. Most were then transferred to my computer at night after arriving at my hotel. I estimate that for every quote written down, I had to read at least ten. This translates to approximately 5,500 markers viewed. And this does not include the markers that displayed only the person's name and birth/death dates, which were countless. I thank God for providing me the strength and perseverance to make this happen.

The quotes are real, the people are real, and their lives continue through us. It is my intention to bring you the words of those who have gone on before us and instill in you a new found passion for living life to the fullest. When you read the epitaphs, please know the words were written at a time of great emotion. With some, the words were from the deceased, while others came from the family. Regardless of the origin, every syllable carries with it the melody of God's eternal love.

"The quotes in this book represent just a grain of sand on the countless shores of our world, yet they provide a common link to all mankind; we are all one."

The epitaphs include those who died at birth, those who lived to be one hundred, and all in between. I have included with each epitaph the person's year of passing and their age. When reading each quote and noting the person's age, you may think of someone you know of similar age—perhaps even yourself. As you read, reflect on what could be recorded about that person on their final day.

The categories have been arranged alphabetically and encompass most human emotions. With each life, with each statement, your understanding of life will be strengthened and a firm purpose more clearly defined. My prayer is for you to embrace life, grasp its beauty and be all you can be. With your heart breaking for answers; it is then you are deeply connected to God, and He will carry you.

God wants our lives to be surrounded by the fruits of the Spirit; love, joy, peace, patience, kindness, goodness, gentleness, faithfulness, and self-control. It is His intention for us to experience Heaven on earth and given this opportunity;

*"We must live our lives with the purpose of growing
our spirits, so when our final day comes,
we can join God in full bloom."*

The time has come; please join me now in the journey of pondering the depth of life's knowledge and be prepared to meet God.

Chapter 7

The Words

"The souls have come calling and may you hear their voices."

365 epitaphs are recorded in their original, unedited text.

Beauty

Bethany Cemetery
Charleston, SC

The flower of youth never appears more beautiful than when it bends toward the sun of righteousness. 1946/16

So complex inside, so beautiful to others.
Perhaps now he, too, realizes his beauty. 1983/59

The night dew that falls though in silence it weeps, shall brighten with verdure the grave where he sleeps. And the tear that we shed though in secret it rolls, shall long keep his memory green in our souls. 1887/69

The music stops and yet it echoes on in sweet refrains. For every joy that passes, something beautiful remains. 1990/32

Oh, I have slipped the surly bonds of earth, put out my hand, and touched the face of God. 2001/61

If God hath made this world so fair where sin and death abound, how beautiful, beyond compare, will paradise be found. 1957/76

Now like a dewdrop shrined within a crystal stone, thou art safe in heaven my dove, safe with the source of love—the everlasting one. 1870/29

Spring wakes the sleeping flowers and clothes the earth in bloom—and spring, ere long, shall come to wake, the slumberer in the tomb. 1890/30

Oh happy people which sleep in Jesus; they perhaps go to their rest with furrowed brow and wasted features, but they wake up in beauty and glory. The shriveled seed so destitute of form or comeliness, arises from the dust a beauteous flower. The Winter of the grave gives way to the Spring of redemption and the Summer of Glory. 1887/65

The beauty of his better self, lives on in minds he touched with fire. 1919/40

Character

Cross Creek Cemetery
Established 1785
Fayetteville, NC

She was remarkable for her unaffected piety and practical charity, and died in the hope of never ending happiness with her Redeemer. 1841/60

Up right and just in all his ways. A bright example during all his days. 1897/35

An honest man is the noblest work of God. 1942/63

*His life was finished. Finished because of the
fullness of accomplishments. 1916/76*

*His sincerity, sympathy, and humanity will be
remembered always by those
who loved him. 1939/76*

*Servant of God, well done! Rest from thy loved employ;
the battle fought, the victory won, enter thy
Master's joy. 1906/70*

*So prone he was to find some good in all mankind. So
quick to stop and heed the cry of those in need. And so
disposed to say nothing to mar one's day that heaven
with love abrim did not seem strange to him. 1922/75*

*The noble deviseth noble things, and in
noble things shall he continue. 1950/74*

*The righteous will be in everlasting remembrance.
They rest from their labors and their works do
follow them. 1883/37*

*Honest, generous, warm hearted and fearless, he won
the respect and esteem of his fellows, and leaves behind
him the memory of a stainless name. 1870/69*

*Just and upright in all his dealings; quiet and peaceful;
full of compassion; and ready to do good to all men,
according to his abilities and opportunities. 1895/78*

He held a respectable station in life, and his character was that of an honest and upright man. 1831/67

From his youth he maintained an unvarnished and moral character, and his strong faith in the merits of a Savior's blood, enabled him to look with calmness and composure on approaching death. 1837/43

A wise counselor, a brave soldier, a statesman of no mean ability, an able lawyer, a true friend, a useful citizen and more than all, a good man. 1907/89

His worth as an active, intelligent and useful member of society, is best evidenced by the general regret at his loss. He was a warm and sincere friend, a kind husband, and a zealous Christian. 1819/68

No pompous marble to thy name we raise this humble shaft, bespeaks thy praise; parental fondness did thy life attend, a tender husband and faithful friend. 1884/36

Children

Weddington Methodist Cemetery
Founded 1826
Weddington, NC

He is not dead, this precious bud of ours, nor even
faded by the winter's breath, but was transplanted into
lovelier bowers by a kind Guardian we misnamed
death. 1899/11

When God calls little children to dwell with Him above, we mortals sometimes question the wisdom of his love. For no heartache compares with the death of one small child, who does so much to make our world seem wonderful and mild. Perhaps God tires of calling the aged to his fold, so he picks a rosebud before it can grow old. God knows how much we need them, and so He takes but few to make the land in heaven more beautiful to view. Believing this is difficult, some how we must try, for the saddest word mankind knows will always be "goodbye." So when a little child departs, we who are left behind, must realize God loves children, angels are hard to find. 1973/8

So small, so sweet, so soon. 1988/0

O blessed little sunbeam, a child of love and prayer. We give thee to thy keeping of the lender shepherds care. 1938/11

Budding on earth, to bloom in heaven. 1952/1

Mommy's little boogie woogie, daddy's little man. God's little angel. 2000/1

Oh! Not in cruelty, not in wrath, the reaper came that day—T'was an Angel visited the earth and took our flower away. 1842/4

This monument marks the spot where what is of earth has been returned to Mother's lap. The spirit enshrined in your parent's hearts and will there remain, we shall have been united again in God never more to part. 1872/8, 5

Precious Son, wonderful brother, gift of God...Our love for you is immeasurable and our hearts long for the day we will be together again. 1998/11

Fly, fly little wing. Fly where only angels sing. Fly away, the time is right. Go now, find the light. We will always love you higher than the skies and deeper than the blue oceans. 2000/8

One morning, heaven bent low, the gates were opened, we were kissed by an angel, and we will never be the same. 1990/1

In this little grave, worldwide hopes are buried. 1898/1

From mother's arms to the arms of Jesus. 1904/0

*Our little one so sweet & fair,
Has gone to dwell with God up there.
Where no stains of earth shall come,
In his bright & glorious home. 1879/7*

In the innocence of infancy, he has gone to Him who said, "Suffer little children to come unto me." 1946/1

*Farewell dear Pa Pa, brothers and sisters too.
For heaven is a happy place and heaven is my home.
I am going to live with Jesus and rejoice around
His throne. 1907/15*

*He gave so much to be so little, but Angels always do.
1982/2 months*

*Under a little mound a flower is planted to bloom on
richer ground. Thus flowers from earth by death are
driven, to bloom more pure an chaste in heaven.
Tears will moisten this lonely sod, sunshine comes
alone from God. 1880/8*

*Our precious baby girl. Departed from life,
but not from our hearts.
1961/3 (Kimberly Ann Maxson)*

*Our darling son. His precious memory
will be forever in our hearts.
1965/2 (Robert Charles Maxson)*

Christianity

**Hillcrest Memorial Park Cemetery
Clinton, NC**

*Do unto others as you would have others do
unto you. 1978/55*

*Believe on the Lord Jesus Christ and thou
shalt be saved. 1974/81*

*He followed virtue as his truest guide.
Lived as a Christian, as a Christian died. 1920/52*

*We are not our own bosses to live or die as we ourselves
might choose. Living or dying we follow the Lord.
Either way we are His. 1998/57*

Then shall the dust return to the earth as it was and the spirit shall return to God, who gave it. 2001/70

Dead indeed unto sin, but alive unto God. 1874/60

The Bible was his Guide. 1873/72

He yet lives in the hearts of those who knew him best. His whole life was in especial keeping with that great and universal law, "whatsoever ye would that men should do to you, do you even so to them." His house was the mansion of peace and his household the subjects of content. 1859/48

Not by works of righteousness which we have done, but according to His mercy He saved us. 1887/82

As she approached the grave, she looked to faith to the fulfillment of the promise made to the followers of Christ, and we hope has left this world of tears for a better and happier home. 1841/73

Exempt from toil and strife, to spend eternity with thee—my savior, this is life. 1855/48

The gift of God is eternal life though Jesus Christ our Lord. 1919/67

In my hand no prize to bring, simply to thy cross I cling. 1872/36

Come unto me, all ye who labor and are heavy laden. 1885/70

For if we believe that Jesus died and rose again, even so them also which sleep in Jesus will God bring with him. 1858/36

No farewell words were spoken, no time to say good bye, you were gone before we knew it, and only God knows why. However, not my will, but thine, be done. 2004/32

Just as I am, without one plea, but that thy blood was shed for me, and that thou bidd'st me to come to thee, O Lamb of God, I come. 1868/31

She now understands that beautiful prayer of Christ, which says, "Father, I will that those whom thou has given me, be with me, where I am; that they also may be one in us." 1888/74

Except a man be born again, he cannot see the kingdom of God. 1907/61

All things change, but God remains. 1992/66

He was converted 4/25/1880. 1924/75

<u>Comfort</u>

Elmwood Cemetery
Georgetown, SC

No matter how smooth or how rough this day,
God is with us each step of the way. 2006/0

In the darkness we shall find light. In the stillness of
God's grace, we shall dance. 2002/72

Lo! The pris'nor is released, lightened up her fleshly
load; when the weary are at rest, she is
up there into God. 1872/31

Mother T'was dark but light come at last and flooded
my soul with its' gleam, How happy I'll be when
from life I've passed through death, which is
only a dream. 1922/55

I shine in the light of God, His likeness stamps my brow. Through the valley of death my feet have trod, and I reign in glory now. No breaking heart is here. No keen and thrilling pain. No wasted cheek where the frequent tear hath rolled and left its stain. No sin, no grief, no pain, safe in my happy home, my fears all fled, my doubts all slain, my hour of triumph comes. Oh! Friends of my mortal years, the trusted and the true, ye are walking still through the valley of tears, but I wait to welcome you. 1890/22

Water not my grave with a fallen tear, let the grass grow green o'er the sod. For my spirit no longer lingers here, but is gone up home to its God. 1859/20

Earth has no sorrow that Heaven cannot heal. 1984/58

I would not live always, I ask not to stay. Where storm after storm rises dark o'er the way; the few lurid mornings that dawn on us here, are enough of life's woes, full enough for its cheer. I wouldn't live always; no—welcome the tomb, since Jesus hath lain there, I dread not its gloom; there sweet be my rest, till he bid me arise, to hail Him in triumph descending the skies. 1843/59

Sovereign of life before thine eye to mortal men by thousands die, yet of our Father's faithful hand condensed as the contrail us through death's gloomy land. Our souls of pleasure shall obey, and follow where he leads the way. 1832/33

Faith and true in his intercourse with society, gentle, loving and unselfish in the sphere of domestic affection, taken suddenly from earth, he enjoys through the merits of his Saviour, rest and felicity. 1863/30

Why should we mourn our brother's loss, since death to him is bliss? He lives again; in faith he died, and Christ has promis'd this. 1853/35

Peaceful be thy silent slumber, Peaceful in the grave so low. Thou no more will join our number, thou no more care or sorrow know. 1922/43

God has saved from weary strife, in its dawn, this fresh young life; now it waits for us above, resting in the Savior's love. 1899/31

Country

Wilmington National Cemetery
Established 1867
Wilmington, NC

He was of intrinsic value to his country in laudable examples, of strong mind, correct and independent principles, a worthy member of society, a warm and sincere friend. Much respected and esteemed for his firmness, his integrity and honor. 1815/40

Brave veteran, the seasons may come and go, but thy name and noble deeds shall remain in the hearts of your people forever. 1900/68

A friend to his country and a believer in Christ. 1950/21

Who gave his life in the rescue of his fellow men.
"Greater love than this has no man." 1917/19

They gave their today for our tomorrow. 1957/65

Nobly he fell while fighting for liberty. 1918/18

Death before dishonor. 1968/22

<u>Death</u>

**Cross Creek Cemetery
Fayetteville, NC**

Death like an overflowing stream, sweeps us away our life's dream, an empty shade, a morning flower cut down and withered in an hour. Our life is ever on the wing, and death is ever nigh; the moment that our lives begin, we all begin to die. 1806/22

Loved in life, remembered in death. 1892/54

Early in life she made a profession of her faith in the Lord Jesus Christ. When death came, the shook of corn was fully ripe. Dying to her was simply going home. 1877/62

To live is to die. To die is gain. 1925/69

She welcomed death not only as a release from bodily suffering, but as the fruition of the hopes of eternal happiness. 1909/59

Death is eternal life; why should we weep. 1981/29

There are two links death cannot sever, love and memory live forever. 1974/82

To live in hearts we leave behind, is not to die. 1939/18

Sadly we own the universal doom, and lay thy body in the silent tomb. Where death that enter'd earth at Adam's fall, holds his dread empire, and reigns over all. Prisoner of hope! A little while; and he who conquered death; will set the captives free: and thou with every faithful soul to Jesus given shall share the endless life and happiness of Heaven. 1857/29

Yes, the Christian's course is run, sealed is the glorious strife; fought the fight, the work is done, death is swallowed up of life. 1872/62

Death has made His darkness beautiful with thee. 1903/60

And I heard a voice from Heaven saying unto me, write. Blessed are the dead which die in the Lord from hence forth, yea saith the spirit, that they may rest from their labors and their works do follow them. 1865/26

He is not dead; he does not sleep; he has awakened from the dream of life. 1902/22

Dying is but going home. 1936/77

<u>Determination</u>

Oak Grove Cemetery
Brevard, NC

*He is the rock on which we rest and firm on that
foundation stand. Divine compassion fills His breast,
His word is sure, and strong His hand. 1906/55*

*An example of suffering affliction, and of patience.
Behold, we count them happy which endure. 1859/38*

*The rose may fade, the lily die, But the flowers immortal
bloom on high. 1932/28*

*Their children do arise and call them blessed. They
walked in all the commandments of the
Lord blameless. 1872/69*

*Left an orphan in infancy without property, he
by industry and enterprise acquired wealth and
consequences. In early manhood and through life
of varied extensive and important trusts, he
sustained a high character for capacity and probity.
He was temperate, just and sincere and a warm friend
of every man in whom he found integrity and truth.
In all his conducts as a merchant and planter
manifested a degree of good sense, which would have
raised him to distinction in any society. He was not
less amiable than useful. He was kind and indulgent
in all his social relations of neighbor, master, husband
and father. He was in a word a man of sound head
and good heart. 1824/67*

*Now his labor's done. Now, now the goal
is won. 1922/68*

*I believe, and shall always believe, and ever after always,
I shall still believe. 1979/28*

Devotion

Oakdale Cemetery
Established 1852
Wilmington, NC

His wife and children were the object of his love.
Jesus Christ was the object of his worship. His church was
ever the object of his concern. 1955/67

When by His grace, I shall look on His face,
that will be glory, the glory for me. 1936/46

Learned in many languages and sciences peculiarly fitted to impart instruction. His untiring labours proved a blessing to the Church. His purity of life, his integrity and benevolence. His devotion as a husband and a friend endeared him to his family and his fellow men; and his piety towards God, leaves us the assurance that he has become a partaker of the promised reward. "Well done thou good and faithful servant, enter thou into the joy of the Lord." 1853/75

She was through Life an example of piety & Christian benevolence. During a protracted illness borne with resignation, she at all times ready to depart, regarding her work on earth as finished with her dying accents expressed her steady faith & strong confidence in her Redeemer. 1837/69

He has gone from his dear ones, his children, his wife, whom he willingly toiled for and loved as his life. 1891/50

A good father. A friend of God. He left a path for us to trod. 1972/90

Thy life was truth, goodness and love. 1990/100

The Lord reigneth; and while we mourn is our duty, to submit with our mourning to Sovereign will. 1818/54

Heaven's morning breaks, and earth's vain shadows flee, in life, in death, O Lord, abide with me. 1925/84

Duty

Cedar Grove
Established 1853
New Bern, NC

Having finished life's duty, he now sweetly rest. 1942/73

My course is run, my errand done. I go to Him from whom I came, and never more shall set the sun of glory which adorns my name. 1918/29

A loving husband, a tender and affectionate father, a kind and sympathizing physician, a loyal friend and upright Christian gentleman. As a man and citizen, it may be truthfully said of him, "He tried to do his duty." He died at peace with the world, for his life was spent in relieving the suffering, lessening the sorrows and lightening the burdens of his fellow-men. 1887/72

What does the Lord require of you, but to do justice, and to love kindness, and to walk humbly with your God. 1993/80

In all the various stations he was called on to fill, he discharged his duties with honor and fidelity. Full of justice and truth, he died at peace with his God, beloved and respected by those who were near and dear to him. 1838/79

He went about doing good. 1952/65

A Patriot whose honor and constancy no suffering could weaken, no advantage tempt, no loss dismay: and in whom all the attributes of true greatness were so nicely adjusted, so exactly placed, that it was not until he had passed in to life eternal that men saw that he had reached the full stature of a man. 1885/42

He was faithful to every duty. 1922/46

In the exercise of his professional duties, he won the esteem and confidence of the entire community. He professed a preparation for death and a hope of everlasting life, and resigned his spirit unto the God who gave it. 1877/61

No ostentation marked his tranquil way, his duties all discharged without display. 1888/43

Jesus called. Work here is done. 1995/39

Faith

Elmwood Cemetery
Georgetown, SC

We have fought a good fight. We have finished our course. We have kept the faith. 1952/77

To live in the hearts we leave behind is not to die. 1944/60

God could not have made earthly ties so strong to break them in Heaven. 1939/71

Say not good-night, but in some brighter clime,
bid me good-morning. 1932/87

Her spirit hath flown from this world of unrest to
repose on the bosom of God. He giveth his loved
ones rest. 1881/57

The sleep of death brings sad good night. And hides
us from all immortal site, but night will pass and
morning come, and we'll meet again in the
Father's home. 1922/70

So long thy power has blest me. Sure it still will lead me
on. And with the morn those Angel faces smile, which I
have loved long since, and lost a while. 1911/79

For I know whom I have believed and am persuaded
that He is able to keep that which I have committed
unto Him against that day. 1890/74

Thou has called me to resign, what I most prized,
it never was mine; Thy will be done. 1922/28

No word describes this good woman like "faithful."
Her trust was in God. 1884/52

He is safe in his Father's home above, in a place
prepared by his Savior's love, to depart from the world
of sin and strife, and to be with Jesus; yes,
'tis life. 1918/26

He died trusting in the merits of his Savior, and exchanged as we believe, earthly trouble for that peace of God which passeth all understanding. 1864/38

Across the years I walked with you in deep green forest; on the shores of sand; and when our time on earth is through, in Heaven, too, I will hold your hand. 1990/67

God gave, He took, He will restore. 1919/64

Someday we'll understand. 1945/37

I live for Jesus died. 1845/49

Family

**Quaker Burying Ground
Camden, SC**

*Our family chain is broken, and nothing seems the
same; but as God calls us one by one,
the chain will link again. 1996/20*

*Dearest brother, thou has left us. Our home is dark
without thee. Thou found earnest care. In Heaven we
shall meet where parting never comes. 1936/59*

*A loving father whose brilliance, humor and patience
taught us volumes about life. He could envision what
many could never dream, motivate and captivate those
whom others couldn't lead, and cause us to now pause
and smile—for the influence he had on our lives calls
for love and laughter—not tears. 1999/66*

She was one of earth's loveliest daughters, and in all the varied relations of life as a wife, mother, sister and daughter, she beautifully exemplified the Christian virtues in her daily walk. Although suddenly summoned into the presence of her maker, her kindred, relations, and friends enjoy the consoling thought that she was transformed from the troubles of earth to the joys of those who die in the Lord. 1845/29

Sweet voice from the tomb. Go home dear wife, dry up your tears, I must lie here till Christ appears; don't grieve for me nor sorrow take, but love my babies for my sake. 1917/35

The family that prays together stays together. 1995/64

An amiable father here lies at rest. As ever God with His image blest. The friend of man, the friend of truth. The friend of age, the guide. 1938/63

Here rest my son with me; the dream is fled, the motley mask and the great stir is over, welcome to me and this silent bed, where deep forgetfulness succeeds the roar of life, and fretting passions waste the heart no more. 1913/73

A tender husband & father dear, a sincere friend lies buried here, free from malice and free from pride, so he lived and so he died. 1877/47

How loved, how valued, once avail her not, though virtues Cluster round her: her youth, her strength, were all in vain. Death hushed the voice and closed the eye. 1858/22

Thy mother left thee at birth, an orphan to smile, or to weep. She smiled not on her infant child, her spirit took first flight. 1858/1

Mother dear your life is past. Your time on earth not long did last. You were not ours, but Christ alone. He loved you best and took you home. 1973/46

Mother is gone, but not forgotten. Never shall her memories fade. Precious thoughts shall always linger around this place where mother lays. 1930/72

One day at a time. From your mother. 1995/44

Heaven now retains our treasure, earth the lonely casket keeps, and the sunbeams long to linger where our sainted mother sleeps. 1920/64

Farewell mother, a short farewell, till we shall meet again above in the sweet groves where pleasures dwell and best of life bear fruits of love. May the dear dust she leaves behind, sleep in the barren secured tomb. Soft be her bed, her slumber kind, and all her dreams of joy to come. 1767/65

*Loving Husband and Dad.
Keep smiling Gentle one. 2002/51*

God's greatest gift returned to God, our mother. 2003/58

The influence of her unselfish Christian life,
the greatest inheritance of her children. 1923/70

Love you mommy! 2005/53

Friendship

Cross Creek Cemetery
Fayetteville, NC

It is doing and giving for somebody else in which all life's splendor depends. The joy of this world, when you sum it all up, is found in the making of Friends. 1927/21

He caught a lot of hearts. 2006/25

His memory will be long cherished by a large circle of friends, to whom his unobtrusive virtues had greatly endeared him. As he lived esteemed and respected, so he died regretted by all who knew him. 1839/35

Loving Dad, Paw Paw, Brother, Son and Friend. He was a kind, sincere and dedicated man who brought joy to those he touched. His lively sense of humor will be missed by his family and friends. We treasure memories of his laughter and love. Your bright smile still warms our hearts. We shared a special love. Gone, but not forgotten. 2000/63

Write your name in kindness, love and mercy on the hearts of thousands you come in contact with year by year, and you will never be forgotten. 2005/56

Greater love hath no man then this, that a man lay down his life for his friends. 1944/24

Help us to help each other, Lord, each other's burdens bear, let each his friendly and afford, to soothe another's care. 1958/55

Why do we mourn departed friends or shake at death's alarm, Tis but the voice that Jesus sends to call them to his arms. 1894/69

Each step I take, each word I speak, each day is counted up. When my life on this earth is over, I cannot change a step, or a word. Let all my steps be to help others according to their needs, let all my words be to bring a smile to each face I see. By doing these seemingly two small tasks, I surely made this world a better place when I left than when I came. 1986/73

She concealed her tears, but shared her smiles. 2005/42

A friend to the friendless. 1901/89

Future

**Kingston Church Cemetery
Conway, SC**

*The hours that part us will bring us together again.
1955/70*

*May her memory serve as a guide for footsteps and light
the path of our journey through life. 1928/89*

*Thy life's voyage has ended. Thy mortal afflictions
have passed. The ages in heaven thou art spending
forever and ever shall last. 1887/67*

*Let each loss that makes earth dreary,
make the hope of heaven more dear. 1940/64*

*Go home my friends, dry up your tears. I lay here till
Christ appears. When he appears, I will arise and
follow with immortal eyes. 1863/35*

*Tell me not in mournful numbers, life is but an empty
dream! For the soul is dead that slumbers, and things
are not what they seem. Life is real! Life is earnest!
And the grave is not the goal; dust thou art, to dust
returnest, was not spoken of the soul. 2001/74*

*Not now, but in the coming years, it may be in the better
land, we'll read the meaning of our tears, and there
some time, we'll understand. 1912/78*

*There is a world above, where parting is unknown,
a long eternity of love; formed for the good alone,
and faith beholds the living here. 1861/65*

*He died trusting in the merits of his Savior,
and exchanged as we believe, earthly trouble for that
peace of God which passeth all understanding. 1864/38*

*Hold her Father in thine arms and let her hence forth
be a messenger of love between our
human hearts and thee. 1884/36*

*They came to raise our hearts to heaven.
They go to call us there.
1941/41*

<u>Hope</u>

**Cedar Grove Cemetery
New Bern, NC**

"Be joyful in HOPE, patient in affliction, faithful in prayer…" Romans 12:12 God offers us eternal HOPE, something that goes beyond what this world has to offer. We are forever blessed because of you, sweet girl. 2004/12

*Don't lose hope…Everything works out in the end. You
just have to look in small places all
around you. 2002/22*

*Hope looks beyond the bounds of time—when what
we now deplore, shall rise full immortal prime, and
bloom to fade no more. When cease fond nature, cease
thy tears, religious points on high, where everlasting
springs appear and joys that cannot die. 1876/81*

*Blest hope indeed that points away, from this low grave,
this mound of clay o'er which I bend me weeping; to
that bright spirit world on high where loved ones never
droop and die, or in the grave lie sleeping. 1858/31*

*Fear no more, the heat of the sun, nor, the furious
winter's rages; thou thy worldly task has done, home art
gone, and taken thy wages. 1968/62*

*When we at death must part, How keen, how deep the
pain, But we shall still be joined in hearts,
and hope to meet again. 1895/50*

*To be absent from the body, is to be
present with the Lord. 1982/76*

*Again we hope to meet thee when the day life is fled.
Then in heaven with joy to greet thee where
no farewell tear is shed. 1892/34*

*We'll know why clouds instead of sun were once many
a cherished plan; why song has cease'd when scarce
begun; tis there sometime, will understand. 1900/27*

Farewell sweet spirit, may thy memory teach our hearts to wait till time is o'er. Then shall we own in Angel speech. Not lost, but gone before. 1858/74

In sure and certain hope to rise, and claim her mansion in the skies: a Christian here has flesh laid down, the cross exchanging for a crown. 1920/45

My witness is in heaven and my record is on high. I cried unto the Lord with my voice and He heard me out of his holy hill. 1922/40

Your smile was our sunshine, your love was our security; your heavenly home our hope. 1945/28

There is no parting in heaven. 1929/42

Look up and smile. 2005/60

Inspiration

Oakdale Cemetery
Hendersonville, NC

Rather than mourn the absence of the flame,
let us celebrate how brightly it burned. 2002/61

We cannot, after all, judge a biography by its length,
by the number of pages in it. We must judge it by the
richness of the contents. Sometimes the unfinished are
among the most beautiful symphonies. 2004/39

He was eminently upright and benevolent through life—and was supported in the approach of death by the hope of a glorious immortality through Jesus Christ! Hear what the voice from heaven proclaims for all the pious dead, sweet is the sound of their names, and soft their sleeping bed. Far from their world of toil and strife, they're present with the Lord. The labors of their mortal life, end in a large reward. 1828/50

His manner was gentle, taste simple, wants few. Was kind and just to all. Had many friends, no real enemies, but the respect of all who knew him. 1902/67

For when the one Great Scorer comes, to write against your name, He writes not that you lost or won, but how you played the game. 1971/22

She was too good, too gentle and fair, to dwell in this cold world of care. 1921/35

My flesh shall slumber in the ground, till the last trumpets joyful sound, then burst the chains with sweet sunrise and in my Saviour's image rise. 1810/22

All the jarring notes of life seem blending in a psalm. And all the angels at its strife slow rounding into calm. And so the shadows fall apart and so the west winds play. And all the windows of my heart I open to the day. 1898/55

Happy is the man rich in good deeds and love of learning, for he shall be honored in life and remembered eternally for goodness. 1979/55

Greater is he that is in you, than he that is in the world. 1992/57

In life, pre-eminant. In death, triumphant. 1922/32

It's not what you put in a painting that counts, it's what you leave out. 1993/67

If you could see me now. 2004/56

Love

Hillcrest Cemetery
Clinton, NC

Jesus, I trust you. 2005/67

They loved him most, who knew him best. 1923/58

Beyond this vale of tears, there is a life above,
unmeasured by the flight of years—and all
that is life is love. 1859/22

Happy is the man rich in good deeds and love of learning, for he shall be honored in life and remembered eternally for goodness. 1979/55

Night falls, but dawn to replace it. Grief comes, but time will erase the pain life ends, but death cannot erase it in memory, love always will remain. 1997/48

The heart of man who truly loves is a blessing on earth. He has God in himself, for God is love. 1972/34

Fold her O Father in Thine arms and let her henceforth be a messenger of love between our human hearts and thee. 1909/46

And if God but choose. I shall but love thee better after death. 1999/93

God gives us love, something to love He lends us. 1956/70

The Christian meaning of joy is not absence of disappointment, suffering, failure, tension or conflict. It is rather that men and women are still able—in spite of trials—to believe that the future is open to new possibilities and that love that comes out of pain has a special quality of goodness. 1987/89

Our love will always keep, for there is nothing impossible in the sight of God. Love your heart. 1963/25

I will always love you...more. 2002/53

Beloved Spirit of God. 1988/100

Marriage

Greenlawn Cemetery
Coumbia, SC

The only dream that mattered did come true.
In my life, I was loved by you. 1997/32

Nor even this hour shall saints charm. For side by side
still fondly we keep. And calmly in each other's arms:
Together linked go down deep. 1853/30

What greater thing is there for two human souls than to feel that they are joined for life—to strengthen each other in all trials, to share with each other in life's joys, to love each other for a lifetime, and to be with each other in silent unspoken memories. 1993/44

My best friend, my soul mate, my love of a lifetime, until we're together in heaven we will remain in each other's hearts. Our memories of love we'll share again, for in heaven we'll never, ever part. Until we meet again. 2001/33

Placing my trust in God I wait, setting my face to the dawn of that new day when the shadows will lift and we shall be again united. 1930/47

Making mention of thee always in my prayers. Your wife. 1956/29

His life revealed his high ideals, a life so gentle— himself forgetting; a love so perfect— two hearts as one. Sheltered as the daisy protects the dewdrop from the sun. 1962/78

Sing and praise our Lord Jesus Christ at the throne of grace for us both, "Till I am there." 2001/80

She was but words are wanting to say what, to say what. Think what a wife should be, she was that. 1911/44

Together Always. 1988/80, 1990/80

Reunited. 1896/57

<u>Memory</u>

Harshaw Chapel Cemetery
Established 1869
Murphy, NC

The charm that in her spirit lived, no changes could destroy. 1960/89

I thank God for every remembrance of thee. But oh for the touch of a vanished hand. And the sound of a voice that is still. 1914/28

And when the stream which overflowed the soul passed away, a consciousness remained that he had left, departed from the silent shore of memory, image and precious thoughts that shall not die and cannot be destroyed. Her life was ideal, her memory an inspiration. 1945/25

*We do not remember days,
we remember moments. 1976/8*

The memory of the just is blessed. 1891/65

*A life like hers has left a record sweet for memory
to dwell upon. 1951/40*

*If my parting has left a void, then fill it with remembered joy. My life's been full, I've savored much—good friends, good times,
a loved one's touch. 2001/54*

Tis hard to break the tender cord when love has bound the heart. Tis hard, so hard to speak the words: "We must forever part." Dearest loved one we must lay thee in the peaceful grave's embrace; but thy memory will be cherished till we see thy heavenly face. 1899/60

*Sweet remembrances of the just, shall blossom
when they sleep in dust. 1885/86*

*To those who knew and loved him, him memory
will never grow old. 2005/37*

The song of love never stills, though the lark is gone, its melody remains. 1997/59

Faith, trust, and love brought many special unforgettable years together. 2003/56

May their sleep be as sweet as our memories of them. 1955/69

The grave has closed over him we loved, but his memory is chiseled with as fond affections as the dearest objects around us. 1842/47

What we keep in memory is ours unchanged forever. 1961/49

Remember and smile. 2004/58

Peace

Oakdale Cemetery
Established 1852
Wilmington, NC

The peace that passeth all understanding is now with those who mortal remains lie here. 1887/67

Safely anchored in the harbor of eternal rest. 1942/81

Father, I will that they also who thou hast given me, be with me where I am. My peace I give to you. 1885/66

*The time is now come my body shall rest, be free from
afflictions, and all my distress. My Soul unencumbered
by this mortal frame, shall rise up to Jesus
no more to complain. 1851/52*

*Why do we mourn departing friend or shake at death's
alarms. Tis but the voice that Jesus sends
to call them to his arms. 1825/24*

*Lo, when the silent marble weeps, a friend, a wife, a
mother sleeps. A heart within where sacred cell,
the peaceful virtues loved to dwell. 1892/18*

*The pains of death are past, labor and sorrow cease,
and life's long warfare closed at last, his soul
is found in peace. 1907/72*

*There is enough known of those who die in the Lord to
save us from excessive grief. Death is eternal life.
Why should we weep? 1916/53*

*The last end of the good man is peace, how calm his
exit. His summon'd breath went forth as peacefully, as
folds the spent rose when the day is done. 1860/71*

*All that he knew was that the years flow by like water,
and that one day, men come home again. 1972/62*

*Peace, all our angry passions; then, let each rebellious
sigh, be silent at his sovereign will,
and every murmur die. 1832/29*

*We ask no other wages when thou shalt call us home,
than to have shared thy labors that made
thy kingdom come. 1990/85*

Like a dove of the Ark, he has flown to his rest from a world of sorrow to the home of the blest. 1946/38

Thy faith has saved thee: Go in peace. 1995/85

<u>Preparation</u>

**Cedar Grove Cemetery
New Bern, NC**

*Remember friends, as you pass by, as you are now,
so once was I. As I am now, you soon will be,
prepare for death and follow me. 1870/64*

*Prepare to meet me in Heaven, the separation
won't be long. 1920/94*

*It matters little at what hour of the day the righteous
fall asleep—death cannot come to him untimely
who is fit to die. 1926/5*

*Look on this stone and you will find our journey is over
and yours behind; think then before you turn away that
yours may end before this day. 1928/73*

Now I am gone, I can't return. No more of me you'll see. But it is true that all of you must shortly follow me. When you unto my grave do go, then glad my place to see. I say to you who will view, prepare to follow me. 1865/98

A time to be born and a time to die. 1975/85

Take heed young friends before too late, when here you see, so plain a case of blooming youth that's met the fate, assigned to all the human race. 1872/21

Stranger do not weep for me. I sleep in peaceful tranquility, but I my friend shall weep for you; you still have life to bear and I am through. 1974/31

Death rides on every passing breeze and lurks in every flower. Each season has its own disease, it's peril every hour. 1903/20

Oh God how mysterious and strange are thy ways, to take from us our loved one in the best of his days. 1912/31

Days, months and years must have an end; 'twill always have as long to spend as when it first begun, loved ones left behind. Remember my advice to love and serve the Lord. 1900/56

My friends and neighbors of you call to see where I do lie. Remember well that you're not alone and may do as well as I. 1818/22

Then he paid the debt, you, reader, yet owe, and went the way all living must go. It is appointed unto man once to die, and after death the Judgment. The God that made the earth and sky, and world below and heaven on high, has ordered all things for the best, to bring his people to their rest. 1852/52

Watch therefore, for ye know neither the day nor the hour wherein the son of man cometh. 1849/16

I was where you are, soon you will be where I am, be ready. 1974/74

In the assured hope of everlasting life. For while she lived on earth, her soul was Heavenward, her daily walk shone with the light of Christian graces. Her words were kindness and her deeds were loving. Chastened by suffering, she grew into the image of her Lord, and her patient spirit ripened for the Kingdom of God. Reader. Art thou prepared to welcome death, like her whose body rests in hope beneath. 1868/37

My earthly body now is gone, my soul with Christ does dwell, prepare yourself, while in the flesh, to escape the flames of hell. 1938/41

I want to be ready when He comes. 1972/78

"I told you I was sick." Love, Jack
2011/74

Servanthood

Cross Creek Cemetery
Fayetteville, NC

She hath done what she could. 1936/68

If one person comes to know the Lord through my life,
then it will be worth it all. 1986/18

He gave generously of his heart and energies for the
welfare of others. 1964/69

*God's greatest gift to mankind is the ability to develop
wisdom and wisely use it to help others. This was his
way of life, and for this he will ever be
remembered. 1971/61*

*In life a devoted statesman and public servant. In death,
a reminder to all to live life for the betterment
of others. 2005/55*

*God takes the most eminent and choicest of his servants
for the choicest and most eminent afflictions. They who
have received most grace from God are able to bear
most afflictions from God. Affliction does not hit the
saint by chance, but by direction. God does not draw
his bow at a venture. Every one of his arrows goes upon
a special errand and touches no breast but his against
who it is sent. It is not only the grace, but the glory of a
believer when we can stand and take
affliction quietly. 1979/47*

*Love for humanity, devotion to friends and loyalty to the
oath of Hippocrates endeared him to all who knew him.
Let his works praise him. 1941/73*

*Blessed be the man that provideth for the sick and the
needy. The Lord shall deliver him in the time
of trouble. 1971/70*

*"Others, Lord, Yes, Others." Let this my motto to be.
Help me to live for others that I may live
like Thee. 1959/86*

So prone was he to find some good in all mankind. So quick to stop and heed the cry of those in need. That heaven with love abrim, did not seem strange to him. 1936/59

Yea - her hands she stretched forth to the needy, And she smiled at the coming of the last day. 1900/64

May the works I've done, speak for me. 1979/66

He lived and died to help others. 1975/58

Sorrow

Eastside Cemetery
Rockingham, NC

We had a little treasure once. She was our joy and pride. We loved her, ah! Perhaps too well, for soon she slept and died. All is dark within our dwelling, lonely are our hearts today, for the one we loved so dear, has forever passed away. 1988/6

Since heaven has become your home, I sometimes feel so all alone. And though we now are far apart, you hold a big piece of my heart. I never knew how much I'd grieve, when it was time for you to leave. Or just how much my heart would ache, from that one fragment you would take. God let this tender hole remain, reminding me we'll meet again. And one day all the pain will cease, when He restores this missing piece. 2006/25

Slowly fading, lingering, dying like the leaf he passed away; heeding not our tears of anguish, heaven has claimed its own today—and we weep. 1897/26

No fame I crave before my God, a simple goal I keep. I hope just once before I die to get sufficient sleep. 1951/19

We miss thy kind and willing hand, thy fond and earnest care, our home is dark without thee, we miss thee everywhere. 1904/32

How many fond hopes lie buried here. 1966/37

Farewell dear daughter and son, a sad farewell. Your loss from earth can tell. Your stay on earth was short but sweet. We hope in heaven, again to meet. 1923/21, 1927/21

Dearest Frank, you have passed from our sight, though the sweet memories of you will live on in my heart, where an aching void has been created, which can never be filled. 1949/27

It broke our hearts to lose you, but you didn't go alone for part of us went with you the day God called you home. 1998/29

A precious one from us is gone. A voice we love is stilled, a place is vacant in our home, which never can be filled. 1938/65

From sorrow, we find joy; from confusion, we find direction; and from death, we find life. 1997/70

Vision

**Magnolia Cemetery
Charleston, SC**

*Death is but the starlit strip between the companionship
of yesterday and the reunion of tomorrow. 2000/89*

*I shall be satisfied when I awake with
thy likeness. 1921/81*

*He has showed thee, O man, what is good; and what
does the Lord require of thee, but to do justly, and to
love mercy, and to walk humbly with thy God? 1978/44*

*When your bright and curious eyes open once again,
only you will know the wonders they have seen. 2007/61*

Thus here endeth the first lesson. 1940/81

*His kindness and understanding will remain with us
as long as life lasts. 1932/74*

*We seem to give him back to thee dear God, who gavest
him to us, yet as thou didst not loose him in giving, so
we have not lost him in his return. For life is eternal:
and death is only a horizon: and a horizon is not
beyond the limit of our sight. 1971/54*

*To every thing there is a season and a time to every
purpose under the heaven. 1988/68*

*As thou canst no longer stay to cheer us with thy love:
we hope to meet with thee again in yon
bright world above. 1975/24*

*Her steadfast aim, the glory of her God, her only trust a
Saviour's precious blood. Such friends of Jesus, death
assaults in vain, with them to live is Christ;
to die, is gain. 1898/37*

*Eye hath not seen, nor ear heard, neither have entered
into the heart of man, the things which God hath
prepared for them that love Him. 1943/82*

*Thou shalt guide me with they counsel, and after that
receive me with glory. 1883/66*

When we all get to heaven. 2004/83

Beyond the sunset. 1994/90

Wisdom

Old Stone Church Graveyard
Clemson, SC

*Out of clutter, find simplicity, from discord, find
harmony, in the middle of difficulty,
lies opportunity. 1997/20*

*Though each man's flight is his own,
no one soars alone. 1996/71*

Life is uncertain. Eat dessert first. 1990/53

*How grand in age, how fair in youth, are virtue,
friendship, love and truth. 1862/81*

*We wind our life about another's life. We hold it closer,
dearer than our own. All on it faints and fails in deathly
strife, leaving us stunned, stricken and alone. But Oh!
We do not die with those we mourn,
this also can be borne. 1922/55*

*He is still living; deeds, not years,
constitute true life. 1897/31*

*I shall be telling this with a sigh. Somewhere ages and ages
hence two roads divided in a wood and I—I took
the one less traveled by. And that has made
all the difference. 1985/40*

God loves all of us. 1996/81

*Goodness consists not in the outward things we do,
but in the inward things we are. 1990/93*

*For this corruptible must put on incorruption
and this mortal must put on immortality. 1837/70*

*Love though thy land with love from out of the storied
past, and used within the present, but transfused
through future time by power of thought. 1934/63*

Today, the road all runners come, shoulder high we bring you home and set you at your threshold down, townsman of a stiller town. Smart lad, to slip betimes away from fields where glory does not stay and early though the laurels grows it withers quicker than the rose. Eyes the shady night has shut cannot see the record cut, and silence sounds no worse than cheers after earth has stopped the ears: Now you will not sell the rout of lads that wore their honors out, runners whom renown outran and the name died before the man. 1985/38

Life is not fair, but you can be. 2001/58

Whether we live, we live unto the Lord and whether we die, we die unto the Lord; whether we live therefore or die, we are the Lord's. 1885/64

And in the end, it's not the years in your life, but the life in your years. 2004/40

The face of the world changed, I think, since I first heard the footsteps of thy soul. 2009/51

Be loyal and forever young. 1996/26

World without end. 1968/6

Young Adults

Greenview Cemetery
Reidsville, NC

God gathers the choicest flowers from
the garden of life. 1890/33

He loved and was loved by many. He was always
searching and though his journey was short,
he knew his destination. Knowing this,
we rejoice in his life. 1999/29

Memories so sweet still linger here, that he gave us in 22 years. So gentle and kind, so sweet and dear. And now for a while we've had to part, it brings sorrow to us, and pain to our heart. But the joy that we knew and the love that we shared, we'll find once again when we're together up there. Then never again will we have to part, and God will hold us close to this dear sweet heart. 1978/22

The tears of absent parents, the anxieties of waiting friends, medical skill could avail nothing. If angels arm could not snatch him from the grave, legions of angels can't confine him there. Here in the dreary grave confined; he sleeps in death's dark gloom, until the eternal morning breaks the slumber of the tomb. We part to meet again. 1847/31

Weep not father and mother for me, for I am waiting in glory for thee. 1929/24

God gives us love. Something to love he lends. No farewell words were spoken, not one to say goodbye, you were gone before we knew it, and only God knows why. 1959/25

In the midst of Life, we are in death. Her sun went down while it was yet day. 1896/21

Farewell! Dear, amiable youth! 1828/22

No sin, no grief, no pain, safe in my happy home, my fears all fled, my doubts all slain, my hour of triumph come. Oh! Friends of my mortal years, the trusted and the true, ye are walking still through the valley of tears, but I wait to welcome you. 1890/22

He leaves the sweet memory of obedience and truth. 1898/18

In loving memory of our beautiful son and brother, whose friendly smile and genuine compassion for others brought joy and happiness to everyone he met. 2004/18

Until we meet again, may God hold you in the palm of his hand. 2001/17

Ah! Why so soon, just as the bloom appears, drops the fair blossom in this vale of tears, death view'd the treasure to the desert garden, and claimed the right of planting it in heaven. 1875/18

Weep not for her who meekly led a life of piety and love, whose unassuming virtue shed a hallowed influence from above. 1889/21

With ample opportunities, and gifted genius, eloquence and good cheer, directed by supreme faith, a thirst for knowledge, and exalted aspirations, his future usefulness on earth seemed assured when unexpectedly, the call came, to come up higher. 1901/22

When God sees fit to take the gifts He gave, let earthly parents, cheerfully resign, their lovely off spring to a peaceful grave and say as Christ hath taught; "Thy will, not mine." 1838/19

Why was it so: it seemed so sweet to have him with us here. We only know that God knew best, some day it will be clear. 1898/22

Blessed are those who remember their Creator in the days of their youth, and die in peace with God. 1859/24

T'was finished; the conflict is past, the heaven born spirit is fled. Her wish is accomplished at last, and now she's entombed with the dead. Her soul has now taken its flight, to mansions of glory above. To mingle with Angels of light, and dwell in the kingdom of love. 1810/16

A sweet gentle breeze has crossed our lives. 1986/30

Some day we will understand. 1938/19

We will meet again. 1911/20

Chapter 8

What's Next?

I hope you enjoyed *"The Words"* that God so graciously allowed me to gather. How they will impact your life is only for you to decide, but I trust you are now reaching a higher level of eternal understanding.

You are coming to the end of this writing, so what's next? What to do now? My first suggestion is for you to sincerely thank God for your life and all your blessings. Second, sit down with your family and tell them how much you love them. And third, write your own epitaph.

Document the *"forever"* words by which you will be remembered by those *"who pass by."* And if you are challenged with this, I would encourage you to visit some cemeteries and do as I have done. When you do, I promise the words will come.

Please find below the words of a few who have prepared their epitaphs in advance:

> *"Remember friend I wish you well,*
> *up in heaven or down in hell.*
> *To follow you I will not consent,*
> *until I find out which way you went."*

> *"Being; therefore, enjoy."*

"Every part of all of it was the best."

"I lived a good life and did my best.
I have gone home and am happy.
How about you?"

"I shall pass through this world but once. If therefore, there be
any kindness I can show, or any good thing I can do, let me not
defer it or neglect it, for I shall not pass this way again.
Love is tender, gentle and kind."

"Shed not too many tears when I shall leave. For my sake, turn
again to life and smile. Nerving thy heart and trembling hand to
do that which will comfort other souls than thine. Complete these
dear unfinished tasks of mine and I perchance may
therein comfort you."

"Thanks for stopping by."

"Please, remember me."

Living your life from the end will empower you to capture the essence of who you are. It will allow your strengths and talents to surface where you can consistently and persistently serve your fellow man.

This will position you to truly embrace life and allow the love that is hidden deep within your soul to come forth as a beacon of light of hope and joy. It will be your catalyst to touch the face of God, while He so gently holds you in the palm of His hand.

Chapter 9

Your Last Day/Week

I f today were to be your final day on earth, how would you live it? We discussed this earlier, but I'd like to give you a slight revision to that saying: *"If this week were to be your final week, how would you live it?"* A day is hard to manage, but a week gives you enough time to do the things to be remembered well. After all, God in His infinite wisdom spelled out in the very beginning of His good Book the timeline of seven days.

If you had one week to live, what would you do? Who would you see? What calls would you make? Have you ever envisioned your final week? Would you be old, gray, family at your bedside and with your final breath, tell them you love them? Or will you die unexpectedly without the chance to say goodbye? What level of spiritual awareness are you willing to recognize? Have you embraced the reality that you are spirit first and physical body second? How will you handle the storm of death when it comes charging into your life?

These are hard questions, but they must be embraced if you are to live life to the fullest. I encourage you to spend quiet time reflecting on these and other questions that surround life. We don't know when we will die, but what we do know is that our final day and week will come and we must be prepared.

Also, in measuring the length of our lives we traditionally use years. As part of my challenge, I would encourage you to start thinking in terms of weeks. A year is a long time to measure, but the weeks click off at a faster rate, and thus is a more frequent reminder that our lives are passing by.

For example, the average age of today's human is approximately 75 years, but in using the smaller block of time we are now looking at 3900 weeks. If you were to live to be 100, then that would equate to 5200 weeks; age 50 would be 2600 weeks, and so forth. I think you get the idea; just something to think about.

Please find below a few suggestions on how to live the weeks of your life and to be remembered well:

- Watch a sunrise and sunset every chance you can and share the moment.
- Write a note of kindness to someone.
- Make a phone call to someone you haven't talked with recently.
- Give a homeless person food to eat.
- Tell your family you love them by listening to them.
- Hug someone daily or give a pat on the back.
- Do something kind for someone you don't know.
- Use the words "please" and "thank you" in conversation.
- Learn something new and share it.
- Share Jesus Christ with anyone.

Another question to ask yourself: *"If you died yesterday, what would you want your family to know today?"* Answering this will require additional preparation and below are a few suggestions:

- A video clip of your final goodbye.
- A detailed will.
- A final handwritten letter.
- A "things to do" list for your spouse, including funeral details.
- A recent picture of you doing what you love.
- A "goody bag" of special memories for your family and friends.
- And, of course, your handwritten epitaph.

I encourage you to consider these tasks and take action for their completion. Your loved ones will be most appreciative of your kind acts of preparation.

"The pain of your loss can be greatly healed
by your loving preparedness."

Chapter 10

Two Fine Examples

Aside from your epitaph, a personal, hand written letter expressing your love for family and friends will be your most valued possession. Recently, God allowed two handwritten letters to embrace my existence; both excellent examples of going to the next level and preparing.

The first is from Linda, discovered four years after her passing when cleaning out her nightstand in our bedroom. I had gone through Linda's nightstand several times after her passing and never found this letter. This was another *God thing*, for He wanted me to have this letter when the timing was right.

I presume the letter was written either right before or after Linda's surgery in February 2005. Once found, I held a family meeting with the kids and read the letter. Much love and hope flowed as we all got teary-eyed and embraced each syllable of every word.

These were Linda's final words to us, and now by the grace of God, her final words for you. Please enjoy.

Linda Maxson's Letter

Plant me over at Forest Lawn—under a tree if possible (you know how "hot" I get)! Take the kids and go on a little vacation "on me," ha ha. Have fun and talk about loving each other and being there for each other. I do want ya'll to know it was a privilege to have you, Mike, as my husband all these years (most of the time, a few times I could have given you away, but I guess that's just life as a married couple—there's good and bad, huh Mike)?

As for you guys, Lindsay, Andy, and Hannah, I am so glad I (or we) had all three of you! Even with all the fights, there was so much more love and caring and being there for each other—you kids are great. You all have great character, integrity, values, and morals and I really believe you guys try to live by the Golden Rule: "Do unto others as you would have them do unto you."

Always live by that. None of us are perfect—just try to be the best you can be. It's been a pleasure being your mom! Oh, and don't forget your sunscreen, and read!

I Love Ya'll,
Inge & Mom

The second letter is by William V. Groome, the grandfather of my good friend Barry Groome. Barry consented to have this letter included in my book, and I am so appreciative. Written when William Groome was living with his children, it was later passed down to Barry.

In January 2005, Barry's home burned to the ground and this letter was one of just a few things salvaged from that travesty. William Groome so eloquently captured the essence of life's purpose. It is a message on how we each should live.

William V. Groome's Letter

To My Children

You have made my life very happy by your devotion and thoughtfulness to your mother and me. We both have been very proud of your accomplishments in every phase of life, material, spiritual, and the rearing of your children.

I have loved you all dearly and my hope is that my mistakes may be as much as possible forgotten or at least forgiven and that you may bear me in loving remembrance for what I wanted to be.

Whenever any of you overcome obstacles, either within yourselves or in your outward lives, whenever you make others happier by kindly word or courteous action, whenever you lend a helping hand to those less privileged than yourselves, inasmuch as you broaden your mind and hearts to rise above prejudice and self-interest to take the long look at life and attain the realization of the brotherhood of man, you will be carrying in your lives what would make me most happy.

I also wish to thank you and your mates for the comfort extended to me since your mother passed on. You made the weekends endurable by having me out with you and certainly eased the ordeal of living alone without your loved one. I could not have made it without your love and devotion, and I pray that you will have many more years before losing your mate.

Dad

William passed away at age ninety-four, and in addition to his letter, one of his favorite quotes was:

"It's a great life, if we don't weaken."

These two letters are vivid examples of going to the next level and preparing for your physical death. The question remains, are you willing to go there?

Chapter 11

Three-Day Challenge

It's not often you are presented with a genuine opportunity to better yourself, but I have one for you. As the story goes, Jesus traveled the wilderness for forty days and forty nights, without food or water, or the television and Internet. He did this for the purpose of connecting with God and confronting the temptations of evil.

Our society does not prepare us for life or death. Most of us interpret our world based on three main areas of direction: what we view or read from the mass media (television, Internet, and news-papers/magazines), what we are taught in school, and what we learn from our parents. If these three sources comprise the basis for your value system, then you are likely to be a victim of our culture. On a very personal and passionate note:

"I believe history will prove the television to be the single greatest invention that has led to the degeneration of our society."

Currently, the most common leisure activity of Western society is four hours of television per day (and this does not include the recent craze of social media outlets such as Facebook, twitter, My Space, etc.). Television is the most addictive and manipulative device man has ever created, and programming over the last fifty years has devolved from wholesome family entertainment to *"any-*

thing goes." Is it any wonder the United States of America leads the developed world in prison population, mental illness, violent crime, rape, pornography, and obesity?

> **"All that is necessary for the triumph of evil**
> **is that good men do nothing."**
>
> Sir Edmund Burke

With this said, I challenge you for three days to turn off your television sets, reduce computer screen activity to what is only absolutely necessary, study this book, and embrace the wonderful spirit that resides within your body. You could start on a Friday night and continue to Monday morning. This one weekend exercise could bring about significant lifestyle changes for not only yourself, but for your entire family.

"We become what we think about"(Earl Nightingale, "The Strangest Secret") and if your predominant thoughts are focused on electronic visual screens and physical things, then you will never be satisfied. You will find yourself battling what we call the "more" syndrome. Simply explained: no matter your physical possessions, you will want bigger, better, nicer, fancier, faster, stronger, quicker, etc. You will always want more, which in the physical world is consistently a temporary position and will never bring true joy and peace.

You must, however, travel outside this box and embrace the fullness of life's offerings. If you were to die tomorrow, what would you do the night before? Would you view the latest nonsense on television or the Internet while falling asleep in your recliner, or would you read a good book or play cards with your kids? The choice is yours.

You can change society by changing yourself. Limit your electronic visual screen activity, guard what you read, and begin a life of personal and spiritual development. Get involved in your local community, and spend more time serving those less fortunate. When you do, the gifts of grace will flow into your world, and life will gain meaning and purpose. This book can be your beginning.

It's been said that *"silence is the only voice God knows"*, and with this three-day retreat you will remove yourself from the physical stimuli that hinder your deeper connection with God-the supreme power. This test will offer you quality time with family and it is from this quiet time in which you can get reconnected spiritually. It will position you to truly embrace the fullness of God's infinite wisdom.

During this time of spiritual awakening, you could work on the items listed in Chapter 9 (Your Last Day/Week) and get prepared. But, more importantly, there are two things you can do that will transcend your life and take you to the next level.

First, ask forgiveness from all those you have wronged.

"We all carry with us remorse, guilt and regret for things we have done in the past, and releasing these feelings can be the most empowering act to bring joy, peace, and freedom to our lives."

Finding the courage to say *"I'm sorry."*, *"Will you please forgive me."* and *"I forgive you."* will release the power of love as you have never experienced, and you both will be healed. And the most important person you need to forgive is **"<u>yourself.</u>"**

Whatever wrongs you have done in the past, make peace with them and move on. The releasing of guilt is empowering and will remove the barriers that have been holding you back. If tomorrow were to be your final day, embracing forgiveness is what you would want to do on this day.

The second subject to address is the following question:

"If you had unlimited time, talents, and money, what would you do, have, and become?"

If you just won the lottery and suddenly had no financial, physical, or mental limitations; what would you do, what would you have and what would become of your life? Your answer to this question will uncover your true passion and may require more than three days to figure out, but that's okay. This is one of the most important questions you could ever answer in your life, so take the time to get it right.

Also, a crucial strategy is to establish and maintain a healthy balance of life's priorities. I categorize these as the "5 F's" – Faith, Family, Friends, Fitness and Finances. These are listed in order of importance, so please keep this in mind when addressing the above question.

Two additional resources to aid you with this exercise, which I highly recommend are: "The Strangest Secret" by Earl Nightingale and "Think and Grow Rich" by Napoleon Hill. Classic publications in their own right, they offer timeless wisdom and will help anyone with self-discovery and purpose.

Please give this three-day challenge a try, and as the old saying goes:

"If you have nothing to lose by trying and everything to gain if successful, then by all means try."

W. Clement Stone

And finally with your challenge, embrace it with the understanding that you are a precious gift from God. You are a most worthy, one of a kind, special, unique, complete, loving, generous, kind, compassionate, devoted, unmatched, wonderful piece of eternity. You were created in the image of God and may your life be a mirror of that perfection.

"The only things that stand between a person and what they want in life are the will to try it, and the faith to believe it's possible."

Rich Devos

Chapter 12

Four Truths + Two Commandments = One Commission

From the experiences of my life, there are four truths, two commandments, and one commission I have come to know and
have a passion to share:

<u>Four Truths</u>

1) **We become what we think about.**
    The law of attraction is as real as the law of gravity. What
    we think about each day expands and becomes our reality.
    Thoughts are our direct connection to the invisible world,
    which surrounds our every waking minute.

2) **We all are going to die physically.**
    As mentioned previously, death is a certainty. We don't
    know when, where, or how, but we do know we all have that
    appointment with destiny. Again, the human race has a 100
    percent mortality rate.

3) **Physical death is the beginning of spiritual life.**
    When death occurs, your spirit, which has been shaped by
    choices, will be released to eternity. Your spirit will then

travel down a road to either eternal heaven or hell—the choice is yours.

4) We live one day at a time.

"Yesterday is but a dream and tomorrow only a vision, but today, well spent, makes every yesterday a dream of happiness and every tomorrow a vision of hope. Look well therefore to this one day, for it is life." (excerpt from "Salutation to the Dawn"). And with our one day the giving of oneself in service to others, especially children and those less fortunate is the true measure of a successful life. That is why we call it the "present."

Two Commandments

1) *"Love the Lord your God with all your heart and with all your soul and with all your mind and with all your strength"* (Matthew 22:37).

2) *"Love your neighbor as yourself"* (Matthew 22:39).

One Commission

"Therefore go and make disciples of all nations, baptizing them in the name of the Father and of the Son and of the Holy Spirit, and teaching them to obey everything I have commanded you. And surely I am with you always, to the very end of the age."

(Matthew 28:19-20)

The Christian faith can sometimes come across as confusing with all the different denominations, interpretations and factions of the church. But as Jesus taught us, the foundation of our faith lies in these two commandments and this one Great Commission.

Christianity is not as much a religion as it is a relationship. There is no greater joy in life than serving our Lord, loving your neighbor, and helping someone else find Jesus Christ. And that is about as complicated as it should get.

Chapter 13

The Greatest Story

We are all writing our story of life, day by day, page by page. I would now like to share with you the most powerful story ever recorded, one that surpasses all others combined. The greatest story of all time is the life and death of Jesus Christ.

Firmly documented in the history of human events, you will find firsthand recordings of the final days of Jesus' life on earth. He was a man convicted of a crime He did not commit. All He did was tell the truth, but those who judged Him sentenced Him to death. Vividly noted are His torture and final execution on the cross. His cause of death was suffocation. If this were just an ordinary man, a criminal by society's standards, then His story would end there.

After His burial, we find additional documentation that confirms numerous personal encounters with the resurrected Jesus Christ. Men and women alike reported actual discussions with this man who was once dead, *but is now alive!*

A select group of these witnesses found a calling to share their experience with all who would listen. The Disciples were so dedicated and passionate about their message that most of them were put to death because of their belief. And this brings us to a most important question:

"Would these individuals have subjected themselves to such hardship and suffering if what they believed was a lie?"

And the answer is no, because it is not a lie. For them it was the most important truth they would ever know, and death was not a punishment. Jesus Christ taught them, and us, the most powerful message the human race could ever embrace—the message of eternal, spiritual life.

His life was so profound that historians used His birth as the foundation to create our current calendar. Just think about it: the entire human world as we know it determines its historical existence based on this one man. We celebrate a holiday to commemorate His birth, a joyous event we call Christmas that is recognized around the world.

Jesus Christ is the most noted person in history. His only crime was serving others and his love has never been equaled. This is a man who is the antithesis of human selfishness and one who can bring joy and peace to your world. This is a man you need to get to know, and I hope you do.

Chapter 14

Farewell

I pray my book and the messages shared have been a blessing to you. May you now live your life at a higher level of awareness and always strive for more understanding. I wish for you to continue my mission of embracing God's love by regularly visiting cemeteries. When you do, and read the words as I have done, your appreciation for life will be strengthened, your purpose for why you are here will be revealed, and your ability to love will be deepened.

We have before us; however, a great opportunity, the opportunity of choice. This is a privilege God has extended to each and every one of us. Human beings are the only species on earth that have ability to reason, plan and make choices, good or bad. I once heard the quote *"If it is to be, it is up to me."*

Therefore, since our success in life is up to us, most of us do make good choices. We work very hard to do the right thing to please our families, friends, employers, God, and ourselves. But I ask you, how good is good enough? How much good work must you do before you reach total success and happiness? The words that answer this question are more important than the words on your epitaph.

You see, the greatest choice we will ever make while on this spinning planet is: with whose will do we choose? Is it *"your will"* or *"God's will"* that shall be done? Do you worship creation, or do you worship the Creator?"

God, our heavenly Father, provided for us the ultimate expression of love by sacrificing His only child. Jesus paid the price of an excruciating death so that we may live. Could you sacrifice your only child to save someone else? I don't think so. You would rather die than sacrifice your own child. But God did! God loves us so much, and when you understand what has been done, you will then be ready for true joy, peace, and happiness.

I pray you embrace the reality of the Christian story. For some of you, Christianity is a bit confusing, or may be new to you, and that's okay. It's taken a while for me to get it figured out as well. But I promise, if you study the Christian Bible, spend quiet time in thought, and make the choice to explore the possibilities of eternal spiritual life, you will very soon find yourself connected to the most powerful force on earth, the gracious love of Jesus Christ, for it is our greatest hope.

"When your day comes, and your physical existence is no more,
just know, as the sun rises each day with its brilliant light,
as the flower blooms with its glorious color, as a child's
innocence will capture your heart, so too will Jesus be
there with His loving arms to embrace you, and
the worries of this world, will be no more."

May God bless you on your journey of life!

The Places

North Carolina

Asheboro
Black Mountain
Blackwell
Blowing Rock
Boone
Calabash
Charlotte
Dunn
Elkin
Fairmont
Falkland
Fayetteville
Franklinton
Freeman
Graham
Hendersonville

High Rock
Jacksonville
Jonesboro
Kings Mountain
Kinston
Laurel Hill
Lumberton
Manteo
Matthews
Mayfield
Murphy
New Bern
Pinetops
Raleigh
Reidsville
Rockingham

St. Pauls
Scotland Neck
Shallotte
South Port
Spivey's Corner
Spruce Pine
Turkey
Wadesboro
Weddington
Whiteville
Wilmington
Wilton
Windsor
Wingate

South Carolina

Bishopville
Buford
Camden
Charleston
Chesterfield
Clemson
Clinton
Clio
Conway
Cowpens

Easley
Georgetown
Greer
Holly Hill
Kershaw
Lewisville
Lexington
Midway
Minturn
Pageland

Pelion
Piney Forest
Prosperity
Round
St. Stephens
Summerton
Summerville
Sumter
Wagner
Walterboro

About the Author

By age forty-nine, Michael (Mike) Maxson had lost his father and mother, a sister and brother, and most recently, his wife. But through these sorrowful events God's mission for him was revealed.

Mike considers himself someone like you who is trying to make his way in life. He has some of the same challenges; such as raising his children, keeping the grass mowed, taking the dogs to the vet, balancing the checkbook, and doing a good job for his employer. But in the course of living he has been dealt a hand that included the death of many he loved.

Death is something most of us choose to ignore with our daily thoughts. In Mike's case, he had to embrace it head-on and in doing so found a place in life that he can truly serve. He has a burning passion for living each day as if it were his last, because it may be. He has in his own way tried to bring you the deepest yearnings of his heart with the hope of making your life better.

Mike resides in Matthews, North Carolina with his wife, Mary Ann. Together they have six children; Lindsay, Andy, Hannah, Nikki, Rachel and Dana. We thank you for reading his book, and may it be a blessing to you and your family.

DVT Awareness

Risk Assesment

Find out if you or a loved one is at risk for Deep-Vein Thrombosis (DVT) – a condition in which a blood clot can form in the deep veins of your legs. If you have any combination of the following indicators, please consult with you physician for an appropriate course of action.

- Recent surgery which lasted more than 45 minutes.
- History of family blood-clotting disorders.
- Recently confined to bed rest for more than 72 hours.
- Restricted mobility caused by long-distance travel.
- Plaster cast that has kept you from moving you limbs.
- Use of birth control or Hormone Replacement Therapy (HRT).
- Pregnant or had a baby within the last month.
- Varicose veins.
- Over the age of 40.
- Overweight or obese.
- History of heart attack, cancer or congestive heart failure.
- Serious trauma within the last month (a fall, broken leg or auto accident).
- Lung disease (emphysema or COPD)

This is a partial list of risk factors. Ask your doctor about other risk factors or conditions that may predispose you to DVT blood clots.

Symptoms

Many cases of DVT have no symptoms, but if you experience any of the following, especially if they occur suddenly, call your doctor right away.

- Swelling in one or both legs.
- Pain or tenderness in one or both legs.
- Warmth of the skin in the affected leg.
- Red or discolored skin in the affected leg.
- Visible surface veins.
- Leg fatigue.

Prevention of DVT starts with you. If you have any concerns or questions concerning this deadly condition, contact your medical professional today and get diagnosed. This information provided in part by The Coalition to Prevent DVT (www.preventdvt.org).

Your Story

If the Souls Could Speak has been quite a journey for us and we hope it has impacted your life in a positive way, and if so, we would love to hear from you. Please share with us your story, and any quotes/epitaphs that have touched your heart, because your story is our story. We are all one in the sight of God.

e-mail us at

mmaxson@ifthesoulscouldspeak.com.

If you would like to share the message of this book, below are some ideas on how to pay it forward:

- Give the book as a gift to friends, family and co-workers.
- Share with your church and various support groups.
- If you own a business or shop, consider putting the book on display.
- Buy several books as a gift for men & women shelters, assisted living facilities and retirement homes.
- Share the book with your e-mail lists, forums, facebook, blogs, etc.

For quantity purchases and distribution opportunities, please visit our website at:

www.ifthesoulscouldspeak.com

or write us at

The People's Connection
P.O. Box 78982
Charlotte, NC 28271